© Norman Stevens

First published in November 2003

The rights of the author to this work has
been asserted by him in accordance with the Copyright,
Designs and Patents Act, 1993.

ISBN 1 874538 18 2

Published in the U.K. by
Old Bakehouse Publications
Church Street,
Abertillery, Gwent NP13 1EA
Telephone: 01495 212600 Fax: 01495 216222
e-mail: oldbakehouseprint@btopenworld.com

Made and printed in the UK
by J.R. Davies (Printers) Ltd.

British Library Cataloguing in Publication Data: a catalogue
record for this book is available from the British Library.

Foreword
by Russell Rhys
Artistic Philanthropist of this Parish

Yet another gem from Norman Stevens' extensive archives of photographs of Caerleon. It is an archive made possible by the enthusiastic support by very many of our community, who have produced from hidden places many rare and sometimes unique impressions of the past. Their support was invaluable. In aiding him in his hard work as a modern historian, this book does not only give joy and great interest to his thousands of avid readers. More importantly it gives a bedrock of fact and testimony to our future social historians.

Having lived in Caerleon for 35 years I am well aware of the enormous changes to our town and realise that this is not all to the bad. Many of the old unsalubrious houses have been demolished or modernised to bijou and healthy homes. Many jobs dirty and ill-paid have gone with their industries, in his second volume he showed a picture of two urchins working for Brades. I suddenly remembered my first job at sixteen when I worked for a tinplate firm in Llanelly, I must have felt just like them. Forelorn underpaid and unhappy. This book is not about strangers, it is about us. Truly a picture speaks a thousand words.

I hope this book is not the last and I look forward to the next.

Diolch Yn Fawr

Previous books by the author include:
Caerleon 'Scenes Past' Published 1997
Caerleon 'Scenes Recalled' Published 2001

Introduction

Once again it is my continuing pleasure to thank all those who have contributed to my efforts to record Caerleon's changing scene. Be it by photographs, memorabilia, information and advice or by constructive comment. Where contributions have been numerous such as schools or sports photographs, showing those that have attended or involved in pleasurable activities, a balance has been made so that the theme of this book is not too biased. Hopefully it provides a popular interest to everyone and will serve as a spur to those who have material, to come forward and contribute their memories so that generations of their own families can appreciate their heritage before items become lost, forgotten or destroyed.

I am pleased to say that where there has been a response of many photographs ie. school, cricket, football, these will form the basis of a fourth heritage book, hopefully to appear in a few years time. For those of you who frequently question accuracy regarding names, dates and information I do cross check to get everything as accurate as possible, thank you for your patience then and in the future. I would re-emphasise that no material would leave your possession, and by arrangement I can copy photographs at your own home, this giving you the security against loss.

Please contact me

Norman Stevens

11 Home Farm Close, Caerleon, Gwent NP18 3SH   Tel: 01633 420187

Dedicated to my Mother
Frederica Marie Stevens (nee Thomas) 1909-2000
a generous, kind hearted, good mother,
whose early life grief did not diminish her will to provide
a happy loving home.

Caerleon

Contents

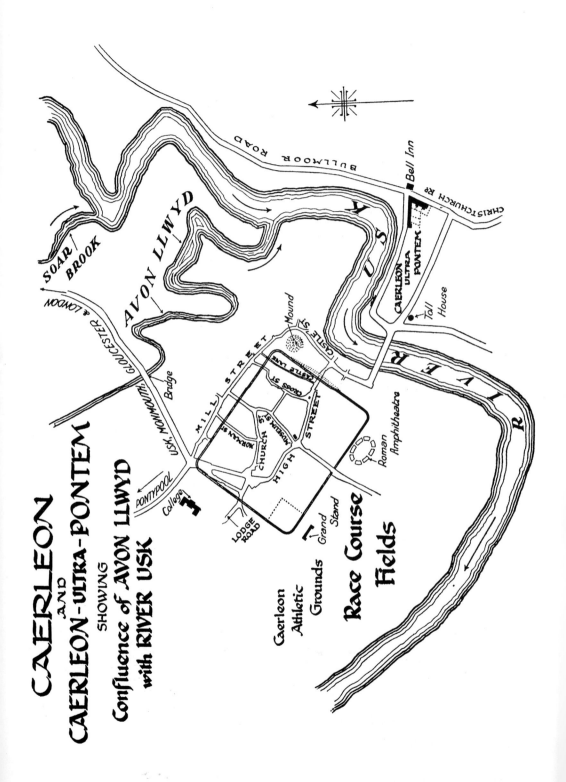

CAERLEON
AND
CAERLEON-ULTRA-PONTEM
SHOWING
Confluence of AVON LLWYD
with RIVER USK

Pedestrian Hazards on the Town Bridge 1965

It's 1965 and Service No.7 from Cwmbran to Newport crosses Caerleon Bridge. Jo Dominy and her daughter Betty Partridge show how narrow and potentially dangerous the single footpath is in their campaign to have a separate footbridge installed. The bus was received in March 1966 the Leyland Atlantean fleet replaced the old style open rear entrance with the new front loading with closing folding doors.

A graphic illustration of the problems using a narrow footpath with two lane traffic. Interestingly that portion of the railings seen in the foreground came originally from the first stone bridge crossing The Usk at Newport which was built in 1800 and demolished in 1925, is it still in existence somewhere?

The Hanbury Service Station

Hanbury Garage before updating in 1999.

July 2001, the site is cleared and excavations checked by archaeologists. Mrs. Richards (Service Station Owner) is looking anxious and hoping that nothing untoward is found.

Completed and open October 2001. The long awaited footbridge was installed in 1972.

Caerleon Social Club in the 1970s with Watneys *'Red Barrell'* displayed on the sign, which was one of the first pressurised keg beers - terrible stuff! The club was situated on the old Bridge Street opposite The Hanbury Arms. Subsequently demolished the site was redeveloped for housing as *'Hanbury Close'*. The vehicles in the front of the picture are a Humber Sceptre, Ford Corsair and Ford Escort showing the fashionable body styles of the time.

On the straight from the Bridge to St. Julian's pub is a Caerleon Social Club outing to Barry Island in 1959. The picture was taken from the back of the leading coach, confident that nothing was coming!

Another large load bound for the Midlands negotiates the turn into High Street. Mrs. Hughes of No.23 and Mrs. Bellin from No.24 wait anxiously for it to pass. The Atkinson Tractor Unit, Number XDW 578K belongs to Bob Wynns of Newport, the driver's crewman guiding him with a watchful eye.

Mr. and Mrs. Bellin's Pharmacy in 1978 at 25 High Street. Notice the overhead projecting sign showing evidence of close encounters with passing traffic!

Bellins Pharmacy High Street

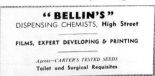

"BELLIN'S"
DISPENSING CHEMISTS, High Street

FILMS, EXPERT DEVELOPING & PRINTING

Agents—CARTER'S TESTED SEEDS
Toilet and Surgical Requisites

Mr. and Mrs. Frank Bellin in their dispensary during their last few days before retirement in 1979. They served the community in Caerleon with their pharmacy from 1949 to 1979. Mr. Bellin served as a Deacon and Secretary of the Caerleon Baptist Church, Castle Street and was Chairman of the local Social Club opposite The Hanbury. He was the first President of Caerleon's Chamber of Trade and also associated with Caerleon A.F.C. and Rugby Club. Mrs. Bellin qualified as a pharmacist in the 1930s, when it was quite unusual for a woman to do so. The bottom picture shows Mr. Bellin at his 80th birthday celebrations surrounded by his family.
Most of the interior fittings and stock from the shop were donated to the Welsh Folk Museum at St. Fagans for suitable display.

1991 and the unveiling of the Caerleon and District Civic Society Award plaque to the *'Ffwrrwm'* Gallery Centre by Lord Raglan, with Councillor Jim Kirkwood, F.R.S.A. and Dr. Russell Rhys.

Celf Caerleon Arts Festival

www.caerleon-arts.org

**Associated with
Mewn cysylltiad â**

www.caerleon-tourism.org

Ffwrrwm 31st July 2002. The back of the *'Manawidan'* Prince of Dyfed Throne depicting the faces of the notables of the area. On the left is Raymond Waller who looks after the cleanliness of Caerleon Streets. On the right Dr. Samuel 'Jeffrey' Thomas. Centre Dr. Russell Rhys proprietor of Ffwrrwm. Below Terry Matthews (now Sir), electronics magnate and owner of *'The Celtic Manor Resort'*.

31st July 2000 at Ffwrrwm and the unveiling of the sculpture throne by Paul Flynn M.P., Dr. Russell Rhys M.D. and Gillian Rhys J.P. look on as Master of Ceremonies Harry Pollaway B.E.M. points to the live rat that modelled for the sculpture created by Ed Harrison. Based on the folklore story of *'Manawidan Prince of Dyfed'*, who captured a pregnant rat when Dyfed was stripped bare by a plague of them. He was going to hang it as an example when persuaded otherwise, the rat turned back into a woman who had been bewitched. One of the nine stories of the Mabinogian.

Raymond Waller, whose likeness is carved on the back of the throne strokes the tame rat, on hire at £1 per week.

The Changing Face of the Square

High Street in Caerleon on 7th September 1998. The National Westminster branch closed on Friday 26th May 2000.

'Drapers' in October 2001 just before the renovation. Notice also that alongside, all signs of the bank have gone.

The reason behind the renovation was the very old wooden lintels that were holding up the front of the building. It was replaced with steel joist beams. It is highly probable that the lintels had been in place since the building was built more than 200 years ago.

Completed and open again. A splendid restoration in keeping with period windows and exterior finish.

The Great Snow 1981

Taken during the great snowfall of 1981. The Square complete with snowman and an Austin 1100 Reg. OCY 610K.

Looking down High Street, note the *'The Copper Kettle'* Coffee and Tea Shoppe frontage which later became *'Drapers'*.

The Snow Fall

Cross Street and on the right is *'New Leaf'* bookshop, now a private house.

Goldcroft Common with three feet of snow on each side and fourteen feet in the centre!

'The Magic Lantern' in Cross Street. A most delightful rendezvous for Tea and Antiques alas only available from 1984 to 1989. The premises are now the Bagan Restaurant.

Beryl Burnell Higgs (Owner) with Billy Sweet (Sweety Pie) a lovable popular gentleman and a friend wearing a flat 'at outside 'The Magic Lantern' in 1989.

Cross Street with shops and single yellow line parking a nostalgic memory of better days. Near The Square *'Budgens'* a mini supermarket, next up is *'Kilvingtons Woolshop'*. Fashion goods are on sale at *'Country Style'* owned by Mr. and Mrs. Leaky. The shop with the canopy is Peter Bevan's Fruit and Vegetable shop.

Peter Bevan's Fruit and Vegetable shop in 1972. Note *'Isca Delicatessen'* to the right. Pictured are Sarah Brodie, Ross ?, Victoria Coxan, Peter Bevan, Sarah George, Cerri Farr and Ginette ? The shop changed to florist *'Floralia'* in 1990. Because of double yellow line parking restrictions this was another needed facility that was lost for the community. Peter first started in the trade as a Saturday boy, working for Mr. Cecil Mills and when he retired Peter took over the business.

The Priory, Caerleon

The home of Miss Ethel Radcliffe, early 1930-1960 Monmouthshire County President of the Red Cross Society.

The Radcliffe family fortunes were largely based on considerable shipping interest, based at its HQ Baltic House, Mount Stuart Square, Cardiff owning and chartering ships for worldwide diverse trade. The Radcliffe Line Co. funnel had distinctive markings of black with two white bands. After her death in 1960, Miss Radcliffe's ashes were buried in the grounds of the house she loved.

The Priory, Caerleon is one of the oldest houses in the county. It is built upon the site of old Roman stables, and parts of the house date from 1180. The wall surrounding the paddock is the original Roman wall built about 2000 years ago and is still in good condition. On the other side of this wall stands the Roman amphitheatre considered to be one of the finest in the country.

The Priory itself has been a private residence since 1450. A *'nuns' court'* still remains in the centre of the house. This is a large, stone-flagged square, open to the sky. Inside the house, a stone-flagged corridor surrounds this *'court'*, and on the walls are carved 15th century figures which are still in a splendid state of preservation, and painted in delightful colours. Set in the walls of this corridor are ancient glass windows which look into the *'nuns' court'*, and inset in each window are three stained medallions, depicting nine Roman emperors who either ruled over Caerleon or visited the city.

On the main staircase stands a stained glass window - an authentic picture of Caerleon when under Roman occupation.

Some years ago a square stone plaque was found in the grounds, and although the carving is somewhat chipped, the figure of a gladiator baiting a lion stands out distinctly.

Anyone walking from the main street along the road to visit the amphitheatre walks along the original road where the chariots were driven by the Romans to see and enjoy the popular sport of bull-baiting. The Priory is now a popular hotel.

Window overlooking the nuns' court.

Armorial
stained
glass
window.

Corner of entrance hall.

The Drawing Room.

To the right above and on the following pages, as depicted in the mediaeval windows of the nuns' court, are stained glass medallions of nine Roman Emperors. The dates are given when in power as Caesar, some only for a few months.

60-59 BC, joint consulship. 45 BC Caesar in sole control of the empire. 44 BC assumed title *'Dictatorship for life'*. 15th March 44 BC murdered *'Ides of March'*.

The Upstairs Landing

AVGVSTVS

To all the world, the Oliue Branch of Peace
Agustus gainde, by w^h all warrs did ceafe
And Ianus temple fhut in all his dayes
Did much redound to his Immortall praife.
Mare Antonie an Cleopatra Queene
Of Egypte both, by him haue Conquered been

27BC-AD14

TIBERIVS 3

A privat life, whilft in Avgustus dayes
Tiberius ledd, of all men wan the Bayes
And to the topp of virtue he did clyme
In Rome, euen all his father Drufus tyme
But when as once the Scepter he did hold
Of mighty Rome to vice himfelfe he fold

AD14-37

CAVIS CALIGVLA 4

Thow neither God, nor man, but Monfter art
whilft thou in life, foe vilely Act's thy part
Inftead of Spoyles and Triumphe brought to land
Thou gather'ds Shells of fifhes on the fand
And whilft in Bedd of Gold, thou haft bin toft
Thy Fame, thy life, and all that's beft was loft

AD37-41

CLAVDIVS

The office of a foldiour once but fought
Vnto the Roman Empyre thou wert brought
And the bloud in Battails wch was fpent
In Riuer Tyber, thou didft represent
But when in Empyre long, thou foughts to ftay
Thy life did Agrippina take away

AD41-54

VITELLVS   9
When ouer Otho's men the Fighte hee'd gaincle
Then oer Italia nigh a yeare he raigned
Idle and gluttonuſſe his dayes he ſpente
On pleasure, not on Conqueſt he was bente
Not thus could he the Empyres ſhores deſer
By treacherie oercome he met his ende

AD69

OTHO   8
To ſacrifiee at the Altar as he came
He thinks of bloud, and ſtriues to Act the ſame
Laſciuious was this Otho all his raigne
By Cruelty and bloud, he nought did gaine
But as by death, ſoe by his life was try'd
By his owne hands this Caeſar Otho dy'd

AD69

GALBA   7
From noble birth did Caeſar Galba ſpring
From others, Fame, not from himſelſe did brin
If he great honors never had obtain'd
Scorne & deſpight, by Baldneſſe had not gain
Cor yet triumphing Foes ſuch pranks had pla
In a lower ſtate had Galba ſtaid

AD68-69

VESPASIAN   preſ
When Rome wth ſword & famine was op
This Caeſar came to bringe them Ioy & reſt
The father of his Cuntrey he was namde
For piety & virtue both enſamde
Great honors to his Cittey this man ga
Tatombe he had & peacefull

AD69-79

24

Priory Dig 30th April 2002. Inside the Priory wall, excavations for a redevelopment are interrupted when evidence of previous structures are found. Stephen Clarke of Monmouth Archaeology investigates the finds. Remains of two structures were found. The first was the remains of a brick wall foundations as shown in the photograph above of a greenhouse which former gardeners recall using and the other structure is thought to be an 18th century round ice house, which former gardeners say was not standing during the last half century. Two early tram rails had been placed over the central void when demolished to support the timber cover, probably then covered with topsoil. This might have collapsed when the car park was created because the same hardcore was found filling the deep void. After investigation the redevelopment went ahead.

Rush Hour at Caerleon Airport! High Street

Early 1950s and an RAF Scammel Tractor with *'Queen Mary'* long trailer carrying a DC3 (Dakota) aircraft has problems with Caerleon's runway. Mr. William Wookey (in braces) is anxious for his cottage on the left. The escort police motorcyclist wishes he was somewhere else! The Priory wall is on the right.

The *'Bearfield'* close to the Broadway circa 1930. A light aircraft two-seater B.A. Swallow. From the track marks in the grass behind, it looks as though it is locally owned and has landed many times before. It has certainly attracted a diverse crowd. Running repairs are being made, thankfully electrical not petrol, they are both smoking!

Formerly Mr. Edwards bakery and shop, newly opened as a café in the early 1960s. Proprietor Mr. Frank Burnell-Higgs is in the doorway with Keith Hurford nearby.

A few years later some modernisation, printed signs and a sun canopy have been added. Posing outside in 1962 on a bright sunny day is Val Burnell-Jones with two members of a Waterboard tanker crew.

St. David's Day in 1963. Dressed for the occasion are Val and her mother Lilian Burnell-Higgs.

January 2003 and another change of owner and use. In 1965 the café became a bank, first the *'Midland'*, now the *'H.S.B.C.'*, The Hong Kong Shanghai Banking Corporation comes to exotic Caerleon!

Saint Cadoc's Church

Porch Entrance, Winter Snow 1981. Built on the site of a Roman temple, St. Cadoc's Church dedicated to St. Cadog of Llancarvon (one of the old Welsh saints). The first incumbent known as Andrew served in 1254.

St. Cadoc's churchyard winter 1997 and the view from Church Street.

Canon Arthur Edwards incumbent since 1995 and curate Clare Mitchel pictured on
Sunday 13th April 2003.

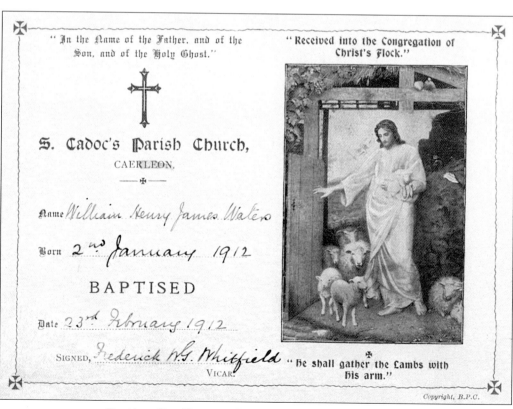

Baptism Certificate and first communion certificate.

Saint Cadoc's Church Choirs

A rare early view of the interior in 1883, showing the beautiful window which sadly disappeared during alterations in later years. Gilbert Harding the workhouse master is on the left rear furthest from the camera, his beard just starting to grow. Compare the group photograph of Cambria House of 1895 further on in the book. In the photograph are on the left, left to right: James Jarrett, Alfred Morris, Alfred Green, F. Gardener and Gilbert William Harding. On the right are Canon H.P. Edwards (Vicar), William Williams Junior, F. Green, Evan Davies and William Williams Senior.

It's 1951 and the choir are singing at the amphitheatre for the celebration of the Festival of Britain. Among the adults pictured are Don Stewart, Leslie Hewinson, Dick Berry, Austin Evans, Douglas Davies, C. Evelyn Gough, Tommy Edwards and Ken Lewis. The choirboys include Len Hill, Tony Morgan, ? Griffiths, Terry Ward, Andrew McBride, Brian Strong, Peter Harris and Anthony ?

Ken (Ikey) Miles. The passing of a loved character.

Ikey in his garden in the Spring of 2000.

June 2nd 2002 saw the passing of a colourful and friendly member of the community, who will long be remembered. Born in 1930 of farming stock with a love of the land, he was head gardener at Llanfrechfa Grange for twenty-five years as well as running his own small-holding. A familiar sight was Ikey driving his tractor and trailer around the area in all weathers, often with his favourite attire in the rain of a heavy sack draped around his shoulders, his dogs always looking inquisitively over the sides of the trailer.

He often said that he would like to be laid to rest in his onion patch but the family persuaded him against that! He was adamant that 'he be conveyed to the cemetery on his tractor and trailer', a wish everyone thought most suitable. His great friend Mr. Ralph Peacock from their tractor enthusiast showing days, came from Grimsby to pay his tribute by driving Ikey on his last outing.

The photograph on the left shows Ikey with his dogs Duke and Bradley at St. Cadoc's Churchyard in February 2000.

June 12th 2002 and Ikey's cortege proceeds from St. Cadoc's Church to the Cold Bath Road Cemetery. Led by the officiating clergy, Canon the Reverend Arthur Edwards, the Reverend Clare Mitchel followed by 500 mourners walking to Caerleon Cemetery. A respectful and impressively dignified occasion which is very seldom seen. Canon Arthur Edwards said *'we buried him with full pomp and ceremony... it was just the way he would have wanted it.'*

Caerleon Cemetery and the interment of a loved and respected gentleman of the old school whose cheery character will be sorely missed. The photograph shows the hundreds of mourners from the packed church at the graveside service.

Circa 1925 before excavations at the amphitheatre (Round Table Field)

A very good clear photograph showing the round mound and exposed walls.

November 2000 and a flooded amphitheatre (itself a rare sight). Dr. Thomas's golden Labrador *'Megan'* looks pensively at her playground in case someone throws a stick! Christchurch is to be seen on the skyline.

Prysg Field (Barracks) and amphitheatre excavations

Circa 1965 and Charles Percival Richards (centre) leads the dig as General Foreman and wielding the pick axe is Billy Sweet.

1927 and excavations of the amphitheatre sponsored by *'The Daily Mail'* dig led by Mrs. Tesse Wheeler. Included in the back row of the picture are G. Wollan Foreman, F. Adams, S. Batt, John (Jack) Hayward Snr., Alec Gill, Ernest Hayward Jnr., B. Kembry, Mr. Williams, Bill Marsh, Mrs. Tesse Wheeler, ? Adams, Mr. Bowen, ? Marsh Jnr., D. Stewart, ? Richardson and B. Marsh. The front row includes B. Taylor, B. Davies, ? Neale, ?, ?, Cecil (Seth) Davies aged 14, ? Williams Jnr., and ? Brown. Young Seth was employed to take the soil away and distribute it amongst the gardens of Broadwalk using a horse and cart. Dr. Mortimer Wheeler (later Sir) husband of Tesse often came to the dig. He became famous in the 1950s for the BBC television programme *'Animal, Vegetable or Mineral'*.

Commemoratives and Discoveries

A Royal Worcester commemorative plate marking the opening of the New Roman Legionary Museum on 2nd June 1987. Depicting the original building as established in 1847, from a lithograph by J.E. Mullock, Newport.

The Capricorn motif edging was the badge of the Second Augustan Legion, being the birth sign of Emperor Augustus, which was based at Isca Silurum (Caerleon) from AD75 to AD300.

The Bull Inn car park excavating the Roman plunge bath in 1979. Curator David Zeinkowitz, supervisor of the dig which was found when Peter Bevan of 'Floralia' in Cross Street started to enlarge his basement to use as a tea room café in 1978.

Below is a Commemorative coin struck to celebrate the 'Isca Festival', the opening of the new Roman Legionary Museum. An approximate total of 1300 copper coins and 350 silver were struck. 900 copper coins were given as presentation pieces to local schoolchildren and dignitaries. They were made by the Bigbury Mint in Devon. 250 were struck by hand in the amphitheatre on the day as part of the spectacle events of the 13th June.

Isca Celebration, Priory Hotel Garden Fair in June 1987

TO CELEBRATE THE OPENING OF THE

ROMAN LEGIONARY MUSEUM

ISCA

A
ROMAN FESTIVAL
AND
VICTORIAN FAIR
CAERLEON   GWENT

SATURDAY, 13 JUNE, 1987

NATIONAL MUSEUM OF WALES
AMGUEDDFA GENEDLAETHOL CYMRU

How the Caerleon 'Scenes' books started.

My collection of photographs and postcards of Caerleon were first shown to the public after I was approached to have an exhibition stand during the festival.

Such was the interest that many club organisers asked me to give talks on my hobby. Demand was high and there became not enough hours in the day. It was decided that a book would reach a wider audience with the advantage that one could retain the images to look at your leisure.

It gives me great pleasure that the people of Caerleon have such pride and interest in their heritage, and that all material for subsequent books has come from residents and families of former residents. It enables me through my books to show photographs and share information which otherwise would be lost forever.

Norman Stevens at his display stand in the *'Priory'* grounds marquee in June 1987.

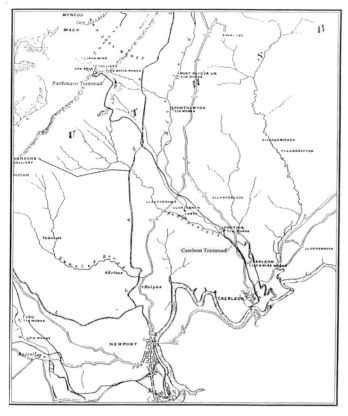

Prujean's Map of 1843, showing the Caerleon & Porthmawr Tramroads, together with the colliery at Upper Cwm Bran, Ponthir Tin Works and Caerleon's Tin & Wire Works (previously the forge). It also shows Llantarnam Abbey, the home of Reginald Blewitt, who used the tramroads to carry coal from Upper Cwm Bran to the wharf at Caerleon. Shown below is an original section of 1770 tramroad rail. They were anchored onto stone blocks pierced with holes, filled with oak plugs and iron spikes were driven through the holes into the rail ends. The wheels of the trams had no flange on them as modern designs but ran on the rail bottom plate with the upright angle guiding its progress. Wheel wear as a groove can be seen in the angle of the end on the photograph.

A drawing illustrating a typical tramway reproduced by kind permission of Chris Barber and Michael Blackmore from their book 'Portraits of the Past'.

Pieces of rail recovered some years ago in Tram Lane, Caerleon. A descriptive plaque can be found on the wall of the Endowed School mentioning a marker of the Caerleon Tramway that was found in the Afon Llwyd.

Caerleon Tramway Railway

Standing in the front garden of the original Endowed School is this mile marker, cast iron post of the Caerleon Tramway Railway Company. The railway was built in 1770 by John Jenkins senior, to connect his Ponthir Plate Works with the wharves on the Usk at Caerleon. 1796 saw the Monmouthshire Canal Co. Eastern Section open and the tramroad was extended to connect at Cwmbran. The wharves at Caerleon were located adjacent to the old wooden bridge to Ultra Pontem and extended down river, one terminating in front of *'Wharf House'* now *'Bridge House'*. After the new stone bridge was completed in 1808 most ships could only reach the south side wharves. The principal ship being the aptly named *'The Iron and Tin Trader'*, sailing mainly to Bristol. It is believed that the remains of the tramroad and of a turntable are buried beneath the driveway of Bridge House and when the Bridge Garage was being built (circa 1920s) a weighbridge for weighing the tram loads was also found. Tracing the route back to Cwmbran from Bridge Wharf is believed to be as follows, starting from there it passed between the Hanbury Arms and Riverside, where a portion of the wharf and slipway can still be seen. Onwards between the Baptist chapel and river, turning into Mill Street, across Tan House Farm (where the remains of rails were reported being seen by older inhabitants) but disappeared when the development of Tan House Drive took place in 1964. Continuing along Mill Street turning towards the Usk road in front of Brodawel House, crossing the Usk road it then followed the Mill Stream (or leat) past Caerleon Mills to Ponthir. It then followed broadly the route taken later in 1874 by the present main line until reaching the canal wharf at Cwmbran. In 1908 the Great Western Railway put in sidings at the tinplate works to connect to their main line. The tramway was horsedrawn on cast iron 4ft length rails to a gauge apart of 3ft 4ins. Some name locations along the route are still here today to remind us of the past. With Tram Road at Caerleon, Tram Lane at Llanfrechfa, Tramway Close at Henllys and Tram Road in Upper Cwmbran. As well as tin plate products, coal won from the drift mines (where access is gained through horizontal shafts into the mountain side), timber from extensive forestry in the eastern valley was conveyed to Caerleon Wharves for shipping to tidal small ports on the Bristol Channel and around the Welsh coast. The marker indicates the distance in miles from the pier! (Wharf) this is calculated to be approximately the halfway mark of the railway.

Caerleon Endowed School

Caerleon Infants Class 1 circa 1905. The boys wearing brass buttoned uniform jackets are from the Industrial School Home at Cambria House, Mill Street.

Teachers Miss Powell of the Infants School (standing) and Miss Adams (seated).

Bring your favourite toy to school day circa 1905.

Caerleon Endowed School

Circa 1922. The back row includes Miss Thomas, Edmond James, Tommy Marsh and Miss Adams. Fourth row includes Annie Marfel, Dorothy Jones, Winnie Phillips, Edna Upton. Third row includes Grace West, Muriel Watson, Mary Williams, Winnie Owen and Ida Turner. Second row includes Aubrey Watkins and Ron Pearce. Front row includes Leslie Ledger, Margaret Rossiter and Dolly Snook.

1937-38. Back row, left to right Miss Thomas, Dorothy Adams, Barbara Edwards, Sylvia Batt, Doris Gibb, Pat Evans, Gertrude Lewis, Beryl Harris and Hazel Cook. Third row Pauline Harding, Barbara Dowden, Isabel Vaughan, Hazel Arnold, Isabel Davies, Mary Singleton, Moira Hussey, Margaret Jones, Madeline Harris, Barbara Trigg and Pixie Collins. Second row ?, Barbara Williams, ?, Margaret Twine, ?, Betty Edwards, ?, Audrey Batt, Gwen Jones, Helen James, ?. Front row Marion Hollister, Hazel Kembrey, Nora Perrett, June Harris, Irene Brush, Hilda Sayers, ?, Gwen Holmes and Phylis Adams.

Caerleon Endowed School

Classroom scene circa 1934-35. Left to right, standing Ronald Hewinson, ?, ?, Evelyn Roberts, May Daken, Barbara Edwards and Isabel Jamie. Seated ?, Barbara Williams (on horse), Betty Edwards (nee Vickery), Billy Williams and Don Strong.

Caerleon Girls 3rd I circa 1920. Back row, left to right Emma Phillips, Betty Hiller, Molly Haines, Louie Davies, Gladys Perkins, Margaret Lovell, 'Romany Girl', Emma Rawlings and Miss Adams (teacher). Middle row Winnie Marsh, Nina Hutchings, Nesta Brown, Eunice Lewis, Helen Marsh, Nancy Williams, Lucy Goodman and Hilda Bennett. Front row Mildred Neale and Molly Davies.

1957. Back row Maureen Ahern, Patricia Dowden, Jane Watson, ? Butcher, Linda Singleton, Janet Snook, Raymond ?, Michael ?, Phillips Hovell and Gail Pountain. Middle row Sonia ?, Isabel James, Merlin Penn, Lynette Avery, Jennifer Pember, Peter Russell, Howard Niklasson, Simon Fry and David Higgs. Front row Lynda Birden, David Treharne, Kathleen Harry, Malcolm Thomas, ?, Robert Teague, Robert White and Carole Goodwin.

Under the supervision of their teacher Mrs. Edwards the Endowed Infants perform the Nativity play on stage at the Town Hall Christmas 1954. Back row, left to right Lee Horton, Nicholas Nicklasson, John Pugh, Susan Derrett, Katherine Hopkins, Margaret Owen, Katherine Bowden, Mervyn Strong and Godfrey Davies. Front row Michael Taylor, Peter Bevan, Terry Baulch, Edward Kinnear, Gareth Edwards, Judith Thomas, Felix Sonake, Geoffrey Waggett and Andrew White. Peter Bevan, a shepherd can still remember his line to this day *'Oh, what a starry night tonight!'*

1960 Mrs. Winnie Taylor teaching how to tell the time. Left to right Ann Smith, Christopher Papps, Ann Bevan and Robert Kinnear.

Endowed Infants 1962. Left to right Colin True, Ann Bevan, Ann Smith, Hilary Rees and Stephen Evans.

Presentation to Miss E. Stallard upon retirement from Junior School in 1950. She was born opposite the Endowed School, educated there and taught there all her teaching life. Left to right are Andy McBride, Terry Ward, Dianne Coopey, John O'Shea, Audrey Waters, Miss E.J. Stallard, Wendy Kilvington, Cynthia Jones, Gillian Thomas, Dorothy Snook, Tony Thomas (homeboy), Elsie Meredith, Margaret Nelmes, Jacqueline Weaver and Stephanie Edwards.

The Endowed Junior School Christmas Party circa 1935-36.

Chariot Races 1992

The Ferrari Chariot sponsored by Giani Zannotti. Julian Burt is on the left and his charioteers show signs of having been under attack from rival supporters.

Representing various sponsors were such competitors as Hanberious Armus, Laticus Entrious, Superius Stemerius and an all girl (maidens) team from *'Chariots'* restaurant.

Chariot Races 1992

Racing chariots thunder through the streets of Roman Isca (Caerleon) as groups, pubs, local firms and sporting clubs bring a variety of hand-hauled vehicles to the contest. All enter into the spirit of the occasion by creating fashionable toga dress which was appreciated by the large crowds and raised much money for local charities. Starting at the Common then to Mill Street and Castle Street into High Street through to The Square and back to the Common.

Spurred on by the lash of fate awaiting in the amphitheatre for losers, an anxious dash to the finishing line. On the right Inspector Julian Knight ensures no one exceeds the speed limit!

The Drovers Arms 1953 decorated for the Coronation of Queen Elizabeth II. William Powell who was innkeeper from 1951 until 1971 proudly stands with his family and friends. Left to right are William Powell, Tom Jones, George Phillips, Pamela Powell, Margaret Powell (landlady), Len Avery, Rita Avery, Lynette Avery, Marie Parry and Susan Parry.

Pancake Tossing Practice - Race held at Gwladys Place

Jim Kirkwood wielding a nifty frying pan as he practices for the coming race.

Waiting for the start in 1965. Left to right Jim Waggett, Jim Kirkwood, Carl Gale and Mike Rowlands.

Shrove Tuesday Pancake Race Goldcroft Common 1980

The winner Bob Teague being presented with the shield by Mr. Michael Bubella, owner of the *'Bellamonde'* restaurant.

The Shrove Tuesday Pancake Race on the Common in 1980 watched by an enthusiastic crowd.

Holidays at Home 1950s

One of the fun events was a barrel rolling race through the streets. The start was at The Square. The photograph below shows it coming down Backhall Street into Church Street followed by excited children.

Left is Ray Llewellyn competing for the Hanbury Arms.

Caerleon's test team on the sports field with the Endowed School and St. Cadoc's church tower in the background.

Carnival Queens

The 1951 Carnival Queen June Harris with her attendants and committee on Goldcroft Common. Back row, left to right Mrs. Phillips, Bill Lloyd, C. Evelyn Gough, Eric Kilvington, William Povall, Charles McLeur and Russell Green Town Clerk to U.D.C. Front row William Powell, Ernie Jordan, Marjorie Williams, June Harris (The Queen), Helen Carver, Mrs. Ethel Radcliffe and Mrs. Jordan.

The Carnival Queen and her Court Ladies in 1946. Left to right Jean Richards, Jean Morgan, Doris Blythe, Isabel Davies and Tegwyn Pugh.

Caerleon Carnival Queen 1959

Sonia Phillips aged 16 was crowned Carnival Queen in 1959 by Chairman of U.D.C. Councillor T. Shierson. The page boy was Billy Teague, Court Lady Monica Williams. The ceremony was watched by an admiring public in Broadwalk.

'Apple Blossom Time' float.

'Mother said never go in the forest alone!' Now you know why! Robin Hood, Maid Marion and Little John! Carnival 1946 alias Elizabeth Richards, Nellie Strong and Eva Harrhy.

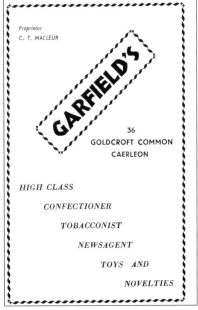

Walkers and horse-drawn float make their way along Cold Bath Road to the Showground 1952. Mr. L. Avery leading the procession and Rex the dog, who was later buried in the 'Drovers Inn' garden.

Carnival Floats 1950s

A Commer Lorry is the float for *'Caerleon's Own Tropical Island'*.

Chiselbury School, made famous by the BBC Television programme *'Whacko'* starring Jimmy Edwards D.F.C. is put on show for an appreciative audience. Ford *'Thames Trader'* lorry on loan from the Star Brick & Tile Co. Ltd.

Smartly uniformed 'Lodge Revellers' Jazz Band on Goldcroft Common in 1945. Back row, left to right Mary Singleton, Edna Dixon, Maureen Bowden, Margaret Wollan, Rose Hayward and Jessica Hill. Middle row Maureen Collins, Jean Richards, Sheila Asquith, Sylvia Strong, Doreen Evans and Pamela True (Drum Majorette). Front row Gwyneth Jones, Mary Waters and Tegwyn Pugh.

Drum practice for the 1960 carnival. Left to right Howard Niklasson, Kenny Godfrey and Nicholas Niklasson. The band was formed by Mrs. Thelma Rowlands and Mr. C. Evelyn Gough. The bandmaster was Mr. Bill Roberts. (Can you play the tune 'Far Away'!)

The 1946 Carnival, not quite the style today but then all good humour a *'Minstrel'*
Guest band.

Holidays at Home in August 1959. Starting on Bank Holiday Monday, a week of events
each with a different theme. Left to right Eric Kilvington, Sonia Phillips *'Carnival
Queen'* and Jim Waggett. The picture was taken outside the cricket pavilion with a
Ford 8 car on the left.

Caerleon Scottish Kazoo and Drum Band perform before a large crowd on the Common in the 1960s. Trained by Mrs. Thelma Rowlands they include Nicholas Niklasson, Mary Jones, Eiluned Williams, Megan Williams and Ann Wootton.

The spotted dog pack of 101 Dalmations as seen in the 1980 carnival.

Lodge Farm Brigade of Guards on parade for the Carnival in the 1970s.

The aliens are amongst us - a queen and consort starring Colin Freeburg and Jimmy Putnam.

1966 carnival walkers with Ann Bevan as 'Prince Charming' and Linda German as 'Cinderella'.

Lodge Hill

Lodge Hill on 9th July 1946 and the opening of the first pair of prefabs, now the site of Lodge Hill Junior School. Left to right Councillor Jack Williams M.B.E., Mr. Slater, Russ Green (Clerk of Works), four construction officials then Morgan Davies, D. Phillips (Surveyor) and Dr. Reynolds.

A tree-planting ceremony by Chairman of Caerleon Urban District Council, Councillor C. Evelyn Gough on the playing field opposite Anglesey Court on 30th April 1968. Holding the tree upright is Mr. John Bevan, groundsman to the Caerleon U.D.C.

Lodge Hill 1957

'Sheep may safely graze', feeding the sheep are Betty Vickery holding baby Julie with mother-in-law Mrs. Lilian Vickery. The bungalow on the right is *'Greenacres'* built in 1953. Mr. and Mrs. H. Blunt occupied it from new in April 1953 and Mr. Blunt is still in residence.

A view of Lodge Hill taken in 1957. The curved wall on the left front *'Greenways'*. Lodge Junior School is now on the site of the prefabs on the left, St. Cadoc's Hospital chimneys and buildings are on the right. Previously a farm track, the road was constructed by the army in the Second World War for access to the anti-aircraft battery located at the *'Fort'* on top of the hill. About to take the long walk down the hill is Mrs. Betty Vickery.

Lodge Hill Junior School 1974. The musical *'Oliver'* produced and directed by Mrs. Marjorie Sheen and John Phelps. The performance took place on three evenings at the school and it was a sell-out, enjoyed by literally hundreds. Two separate casts were formed and used, many children playing other roles in each performance. The cast left to right were Shane Owen, Craig Andrews (Fagin), Steven Blackmore (Artful Dodger), Jane Price (Oliver in opposite cast), Jonathan Clarke, Rachel Gray (Nancy), Lyn Harris, Keith Davies (Oliver), Carole Scannel, Stephen Rooke, Julia Higgs, Alan Dean and Andrew Butcher.

Left to right are Stephen Parsons, Ian Baker, Tracy Pugh (Nancy) and Shane Carey (Bill Sykes).

Lodge Hill Primary Infants School - Lodge Hill Junior School

Lodge Hill Primary Infants School in October 1995. The last day for Mrs. Betty Vickery who was retiring after 24 years of service as a dinner lady and friend to thousands of children. Back row, left to right Georgina Sheehy, Mrs. Betty Vickery and Kirsty Slater. Fourth row Dane Blaby, Zoe Miller and Alex Dare. Third row Kristian Thomas, Dean Jones, James Lloyd, Emma Hazelhurst, and Rhys Macey. Second row James Olivier, Charlotte Bright, Mathew Hazelhurst, Joshua Roberts and David Thomas. Front row Barnaby Steward and Martin Eyles.

Lodge Hill Junior School Silver Jubilee Celebrations 1977. Back row, left to right Head Teacher Mr. Frank Harding, a student teacher, Darren Grew, Stephen Massey, John Buckland, Jonathan Pugh, Graham Thomas, Richard Jones, Karl Evans, David Johnson and Dawn John teacher. Third row Ian Brunning, Richard Knight, Emma Samuel, Janet Peel, Helen Charles, Jackie Llewellyn, ?, ?. Second row Amanda Jackson, Dawn Pavis, Kate Butler, Helen Hayes, Gaynor Wilkins, Pauline Bufton, Sarah Hopkins and Diane Charles. Front row Simon Jenkins, Mark Waite, Christopher Purnell, Richard Wheelan, Nigel Evans and Chris Kingston.

Lodge Hill Junior School in 1978-79. Back row, left to right Mrs. Dawn John, Christopher Price, Paul Parsons, David Coldrick, Timothy Jones, Paul Griffiths, John Mably, Justin Harry and James Pearce. Third row Tim ?, Alshley ?, Alison Orford, Helen Davies, Helen Ackerman, Jane Cantello, Esther Clarke, ?, Gareth Hancock. Second row Ceri Smith, Catherine Stevens, Clare McGloughlan, Sarah Lawday, Sarah George, Tracey Curnuck, Alice Butler and Imogen Sharpe. Front row Paul Hancock, David Hills, Adrian Marshall, Anthony Scrivens, ? Garret and Darrell Gregg.

The School Recorder Orchestra in 1980, Winners of the Sid Tonge Cup at the Cheltenham Music Festival for Schools. Back row includes Sarah George, Tracy Curnock, Ceri Smith, Alice Butler, Stella Benavides, Imogen Sharpe, ? Bishop and Catherine Griffiths. Middle row: Rachel Hopkins, Amanda Edwards, Catherine Stevens, Esther Clarke, Julia Morgan, Laura Burt, Helen Ackerman, Paul Griffiths, Jane Cantello, Alison Orford, Clare McGloughlan and Jeanette Smith. Front row Susan Hills, Sian Clarke, Rachel Evans, Alison Wilkins, Sarah ? and Catherine Byard.

Broadwalk circa 1950s, street lighting by gas and no cars! and the front gardens give privacy.

Tel. 258 Caerleon. PENRY HOUSE, THE COMMON, Est. 1870.

Caerleon, *Nov 9* 1948

M⁰ 7 Griffin

Vorda Station St Caerleon

Dr. to **H. BAULCH,**
(Late W. H. BAULCH & SON.)

Builder & Undertaker, Monumental Sculptor in Granite, Marble & Stone.
ALL NEW AND REPAIRING WORK EXECUTED NEATLY AND PROMPTLY. ESTIMATES FREE ON APPLICATION.

1948

Nov 1st To fully moulded & waxed Elm Coffin, wadded, lined, & frilled, heavy Silver Casket Mounts, Breastplate engraved, & Robe, & attendance with Motor Hearse two Cars & Bearers, to Christchurch Church, & return, per the late Mrs Mary Ann Davis 23 0

Burial Fees paid. 3 5

Nurse Cooper for services rendered 10

26 15

Invoice from a local tradesman who operated from the former Methodist Church on Goldcroft Common.

Christmas and a convivial scene at the Goldcroft Inn in the late 1940s. Simonds Beer was 7d (3p) per pint. Left to right are Beatrice Vaughan (nee Jones), Ray Gibbens, Victor Heslop, Jerry ?, Dennis Heslop.

Next door to the Goldcroft Inn was Garfields Newsagents in the days when it was safe to leave a cigarette dispenser outside for patrons to use when the shop was closed.

Station Road in the 1970s and it must be a Monday as Gino's is closed! The two cars in the picture are a Singer Gazelle and an Austin Maestro.

Station Road, Junction Usk Road and Mill Street. A Triumph Dolomite, Singer Gazelle and Ford Escort show the shapes of the time during the 1970s.

Station Road - the home of John and William Banner

1906 the houses are completed and occupied. William in *'Fairfield'* on the right and John in *'Hillgrove'* on the left. No pavement and the roadway has not been surfaced though gas lamps have been installed.

'Woolstapler and Fellmonger Business'

Started by brothers John and William Banner and later run by Ernest Banner skins were brought from local slaughterhouses, the wool was graded and sent to woollen factories. The cured skins were sent for making into gloves and handbags etc. Several of the family worked in the business together with some of the locals totalling 10 to 12 altogether. It was said that despite the smelly and dirty type of work it was, few ever left for other employment. Ernest Banner once appeared on the BBC television programme *'What's My Line'* and beat the panel, none knew what a 'fellmonger' was.

On the left are Mr. and Mrs. John Banner pictured outside *'Hillgrove'* in 1927.

William Banner - 'Woolstapler & Fellmonger'

William Banner at his premises on Usk Road examining the sheepskins. The premises for processing were off the Usk Road from Caerleon, approximately 200 yards from the crossroad that starts on the right. The gate access can still be seen leading down to the Afon Llwyd river.

William Banner examines stored wool before bailing for sale. The Banner family were in business from 1905 to 1965.

Joan Bevan in 1963 who was the district nurse for Caerleon and served the community for 12 years. She became a nursing officer in 1975. A lot of local people have literally been through her capable hands and have been very grateful for her loving care and expertise. Joan did her training at Llandough Hospital, Cardiff 1941-44. She qualified as a SRN in November 1944. As a teenager living at Pontygwaith (Bridge of Work) she served in the ARP from 1938-41 and is a Member of the Royal College of Nursing.

The Christmas present delivery service by popular demand. This service has thrilled and excited thousands of children over many years and the photograph above shows Santa with his little helpers in 1982. Father Christmas is Ray Williams, the elf is Julie Bingham with Alice Butler, Jeanette Smith and Stella Benavides. The event is organised by the carnival committee, Chairman Lyn Astbury, Secretary Dorothy Astbury with the assistance of Paul Winterfeld and Caerleon scouts to raise monies for local charities.

16th November 2002 - Gino's Day to retire after 51 years

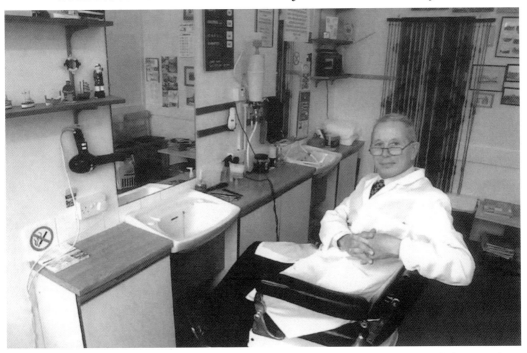

A local character well thought of but now it's time to trim the hedges and the grass!

This picture shows Gino handing over the keys to Joanne Knowlton, a local girl whose family has lived in Caerleon for generations. Gino's family originally came from Italy in 1876. His father was a mosaic floor tiler and Gino's two brothers followed into the profession. Gino's mother who was fed up with all the dirty working clothes insisted that he had a clean job.

Caerleon Railway Station

The approach road to the station in 1962. Caerleon Station was opened in December 1874 by the Pontypool, Caerleon and Newport Railway Co. Ltd which was absorbed by the Great Western Railway Company and closed by British Railways in April 1962.

The station building forecourt seen from the goods yard gate.

Caerleon Railway Station 1905

Caerleon Railway Station from a postcard posted at 9 p.m. on July 27th 1905 at Caerleon. In the top right houses are under construction on Station Road. The two shown are being built for Messrs. William and John Banner. In 1899 they were listed as fellmongers of Museum Street. William occupied *'Fairfield'* and John *'Hillgrove'*. Both still carry the same names today. The reverse of the card is addressed to A. Baulch and it reads *'This is a view of our houses not completed yet. Love from Ernie and Baby Ronie Hope you are quite well, Love from Lucie'*. John and William were still in occupation in 1937 when Kelly's Directory for that year gave their business as Wool Staplers and Fellmongers on the Usk Road. If you look carefully at the left hand platform a young boy is using the shelter of the stone wall oblivious that his need for the call of nature has been recorded for posterity. I wonder who he was?, his friend waits patiently on the platform.

Approaching St. Cadoc's Hospital service ducts bridge on the down line in 1960. Lodge Road Bridge is in the background. The two walkers on the other line don't seem too concerned about the danger.

It's 1958 and a GWR Sidetank 0-6-2 Engine 5645 slowly draws its train of loose couple trucks up the St. Cadoc's incline towards the station. The fireman has worked hard to keep a full head of steam with the roar of the engine's effort reverberating in the cutting.

A photograph looking down on the station from Caerleon-Ponthir Road Bridge with Lodge Road Bridge behind the transit shed.

The station buildings and goods yard in 1960 with a train entering the up (North) platform. At the top of the embankment recently-built bungalows of The Lansdowne Road Development (2003, the road is still not adopted!). Those who had access via the back gates to the station were granted *'way leave'* on payment of 1 shilling (5p) per annum.

1960 and GWR 4993 *'Dalton Hall'* runs through with a van fit freight train. The white painted stones on the banking are the staff's efforts in station pride.

Entering Caerleon from Newport. A domestic coal wagon with access side flap down ready for unloading into sacks for local distribution is stored in the goods yard.

A King comes to Caerleon

A Northern Express GWR *King Class* locomotive making light work of the incline, passing St. Cadoc's cutting and about to enter Caerleon Station in April 1962. Non stop with a full boiler of steam, blowing off from safety valves and whistling warning of its approach to unwary passengers near the platform edge.

April 1962 and the long curve into Caerleon Station from Ponthir and the North with British Rail diesel *'Warship'* class D800 carrying the name *'Sprightly'* coasting down towards Caerleon Station with a ten-carriage express train. The practice of regularly clearing embankments was still carried on although the fire risk has diminished with the withdrawal of hot cinder coal fired steam engines and the new era of diesel motive power.

'Hymek' diesel hydraulic locomotive of Western Region design has passed through the station and under the road-bridge to Ponthir in 1962.

In 1961 a GWR 5015 *'Kingswear Castle'* enters the cutting before passing under the Caerleon-Ponthir road-bridge near the Star Brickworks. Plate layers gang work on line maintenance, no high visibility jackets in those days. The split points rail is a safety feature, in case of a freight train breaking away, it diverts them off the line instead of running through to the station.

Looking towards Lodge Road overbridge and Newport. The down platform has been removed, the up platform overgrown, with the station yard showing signs of redevelopment with units and the goods shed still intact.

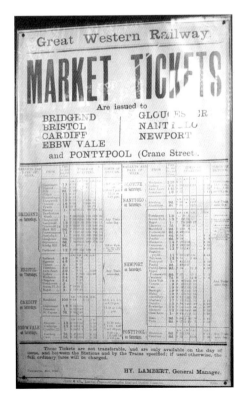

Its 1960 and Glyn Teague and Jeff Lloyd pose for the camera while waiting for the Newport train. On the right is a GWR advert for market tickets, issued by Paddington in May 1890. A Caerleon 3rd class return to Newport on Saturday 6d (2$\frac{1}{2}$p), leaving on the 08.58 train and return by any train the same day.

The last days of the Harris family motor business. Car Sales and Servicing with MOT available. No petrol or diesel fuel sales now.

A proud day for Michael Jeffrey on 1st October 2001. A local boy acquires the former Ponthir Service Station, trading as *'Drive In Plus'*. His dedicated hard work and saving resulted in a long cherished ambition being fulfilled.

Star Brick and Tile Co.

A controlled explosion demolishes a distinctive landmark from the skyline. At 190 feet high and marked *'Star Bricks'*, vertically together with the *'Star'* logo it had been a familiar sight for many years. Below shows it dropping into the space between other buildings.

The . . .
Star Brick & Tile
COMPANY, LIMITED,
CAERLEON, Mon.

The paddock field at the rear of Tram Lane with Usk Road behind the stable block in 1980.

Severe flooding from the Afon Llwyd. The site has now been developed for housing namely Cambrian Close and Centurian Gate.

CAERLEON GAS COMPANY LIMITED.

Caerleon Gas Company Ltd. was founded in 1848 by local patronage and financed by local people. In 1902 after 26 years it was purchased by the 'Newport Gas Company' which was empowered by an Act of Parliament to do so. Subsequently after nationalisation it became the South Wales Gas Board. Above is part of the original brass plaque that was displayed outside the entrance to the company's premises.

Caerleon Gas Works, an aerial view taken in 1938. From the boundary wall left to right is the house vegetable garden, the long round top structure being the filter beds. The pitched roof building is the retort house where gas was made and the storage gas holder circular structure, the superintendent's residence. Running adjacent to the boundary can be seen the track bed of the Caerleon Tramway. The long building alongside is a wooden bungalow. In 1902 a gas supply main pipe was laid from the Crindau Gas Works in Newport along Pillmwr Lane to Caerleon, after this Caerleon became a storage and supply facility station.

The Meter Book

The Meter Book for 1869 and specimen pages, one for The Red Lion Inn and one for St. Cadoc's Church. Previous to meters being installed in premises, gas payments were based on how many *'lights'* were in each building without limit on use! After meters were fitted consumption probably was reduced! In its early years there was a saying *'Caerleon gas, yes you must light a candle to find it'*! One must presume that pressure was somewhat low on occasions. Mr. Leslie Hewinson, the Gas Company Employee charged with amongst his several duties was responsible for lighting and shutting off the street lamps each night and morning. There are recorded memories of him walking his round of the streets of Caerleon with his long pole and returning the next morning with his ladder to examine and repair any defective lamps, showing how thoroughly he carried out his duties. The charge to Caerleon Urban District Council was sixpence (2^1/2p) per lamp per night. The added benefit to householders using gas for lighting was it also generated a surprising amount of heat as well as a welcome bright white light.

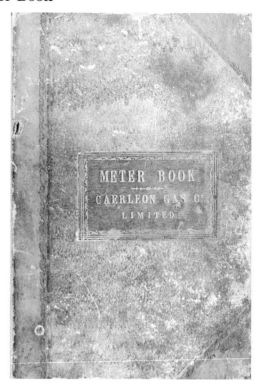

Below are pages for The Red Lion Inn on the left and St. Cadoc's Church on the right.

Caerleon Gas Company Limited

'Gas Works House', the superintendent's residence in the Gas Works grounds.

Right: Mr. Charles Hewinson resident company gas inspector and his wife Agnes. This photograph was taken in 1912. Charles was in charge from 1911 until his retirement in 1935. He was born in 1873 and died in 1948, a man obviously proud of his position and uniform.

Below: Mr. Charles Hewinson inspecting the gas holder, circa. 1932.

Charles in retirement with his sons

Circa 1945 Sons Hedley, Leslie and Vincent stand proudly behind their father and mother. Leslie took over from his father as superintendent of Caerleon distribution station in 1935. Leslie was born in Newport in 1899 and worked in the gas industry for 43 years. 28 of these being resident supervisor, living in the provided house (still existing) located in Gas Works Lane (now Yew Tree Lane). Amongst his other duties was the maintenance of the street lighting and *'lamplighter'*. He served with the Monmouthshire Regiment from 1914 and was captured at Ypres in 1917. After demobilisation he worked for some time in the tin works before joining the gas company. He was a member of the Caerleon Branch of the Royal British Legion for 40 years, 15 years as Secretary and 4 years as President.

THE MONMOUTHSHIRE REGIMENT

Leslie on joining up in 1914. A poignant note on the back of the photograph reads *'reported missing'*.

Taken in the house garden in 1938 Mrs. Edith Hewinson, Mr. Leslie Hewinson and sons Aubrey (Raymond) and Ronald.

Staff of Twin Oaks Sawmills, Usk Road

Sitting on a *'tree in the round'* are employees of Gibbens Bros (Caerleon) Ltd. Left to right are John Murison (driver), ?, ?, Reg Greedy (sawyer). Seated: Fred Adams (driver), Sid Jones (sawyer), Austin Hopkins, Bert Lee (carpenter), ? and Ossie Penn (general handyman).

Top right shows the exterior view of the sawmill sheds, circa 1960s. The rest of the photographs show an exhibition of wood products displayed at Carnival Field in August 1965.

Caerleon Workhouse *'Cambria House'*

Circa 1895, the first superintendent (workhouse master), Gilbert William Harding with beard and his wife Mary Priscilla Harding (Matron) to his right wearing the black dress. Both universally esteemed by inmates and authority. *'Father was a quiet kindly man, who did consider people's human feelings'*. These were the grandparents of the television personality Gilbert Harding of *'What's My Line'* fame in the 1950s.

Basque Refugees occupants of Cambria House in 1937

Basque children evacuated to Wales from the conflict of the Spanish Civil War seen in late 1937. Cambria and Vale View Houses. A programme of rescue was supported by Monmouthshire County Council, the South Wales Miners Federation and by the local Caerleon residents. The refugee inhabitants always referred to themselves as a *'colony'* in Caerleon.

Cambria House - Basque Staff and Visitors

Back row, left to right: ?, visitor, visitor, ?, ?. Seated: ?, House Cook Mrs. Sanch, visitor, Mrs. Maria Fernandez, visitor and Mrs. Crocker. Visitors from Cwmbran regularly every Sunday came to offer sympathetic support which was most appreciated. Even today in 2003 many remember the kindness shown by the local population and the people of Wales.

1988 and a happy band of former refugees celebrate with a reunion in Caerleon at the home of Maria Fernandez, Camelot Court. Pride in her land of birth is shown by the house name on the wall the cast sign reads *'Euzkadi'* (Land of the Basques). Pictured left to right are Maria Luisa Encinas, Marie Dabadie, Cyril Cule (translator and teacher), Senor Jose Antonia Asencor, Charito Juarrero, Maria Rosa Mamblona, Lidia ?, Josephine Alvarez, ? Rodrigo, Enrique Rodrigo, Maria Belso, Pepe Rodrigo, Mrs. Maria Fernandez, Paula Felipa, Angelita Felipa, Rosita Felipa, Ivor (husband of Paula) and Mr. Cooper.

'The Mynde' Caerleon

Tom Edwards

A Christmas card with seasons greetings and two illustrations which was by Dr. Atwood Thorne in the early 1930s to Tom Edwards who worked as a gardener at the Mynde. Dr. Thorne was adamant that Monmouthshire was in England!

A drawing by E.J. Mayberry of The Mound (or Norman Mote) with its spiral path to the top and its tunnel entrance. Cecil Davies remembers the horse and cow, the doctor rode the horse and the cow was kept for milk. It later became difficult to control and spent its later years at Tan House Farm. Cecil's father was a councillor and a friend of the doctor and shortly before the doctor's death, Cecil says the Mynde was offered as a gift to the Urban District Council to be used as parkland (the public previously having access to picnic) but they refused the offer!

'The Mynde' Caerleon circa 1885 previously known as Castle Villa. The castle-like boundary wall surrounding was built in 1820 by the then occupier Mr. John Jenkins, who also owned the Caerleon Tinplate Works. He had concern for his property's security, because of the rise of the Chartist riots.

Mr. Morgan Davies, born in 1876 and his wife Mrs. Cecelia Mary Davies standing outside St. Cadoc's Church. Mr. Davies served for many years on the Caerleon Urban District Council and was Chairman during 1931, 1936, 1943 and 1949. He died in 1962.

Below: Standing in the porch of the family home, Tan House Farm in 1922. Mrs. Cecelia Mary Davies with three of her eventual eleven children. Left to right Molly Davies, Cecil (Seth) Davies and Gladys Davies.

An auction sale poster notice of Sale of the Property in 1837.

Tan House Farm

The front of Tan House Farm, fronting onto Castle Street which was demolished in 1964 to make way for housing development of Tan House Drive. The lady standing outside the gate is Mrs. Jennet Gough nee Davies, daughter of Mr. Morgan Davies who took over from his father. He came from Talybont on Usk and rented the farm from the Mackworth Estate. The land the house was built on was originally the Tan Yard.

Near the house location, the only relic of the past is the capped gate pillar and some of the boundary wall seen to the right of the directional warning arrow sign. Originally the wall projected further forward but a large slice of the garden was lost during the 1939-45 war when a one-way road system and widening was introduced. The stone wall was rebuilt closer to the house.

A view of Tan House Farm from the rear

A side and rear view of Tan House Farm in the 1960s from a water colour painting by Edward Wilkinson. Notice the distinct separate buildings, the original farm house and tannery with the pantile and the slate roof of the later built house that fronted onto Castle Street.

Below: A water colour painting by local artist Wilfred Wilson depicting the rear of Tan House Farm and buildings confirmed as true to life by Molly Davies in 2003.

1976 Castle Street looking towards the future 'Castle Mews' site. No pavements at this time.

A sad and protesting Mr. Bert Pugh standing in the garden of his home, No.2 Uskside Cottages, Castle Street in June 1976. Built before 1800 it was demolished in 1981 when the land was sold for development into houses, now Castle Mews.

Mr. Pugh operated his own lorry as a haulage contractor for many years and proud of his brand new Dodge tipper lorry here, photographed behind Uskside Cottages in the 1950s. He had contracts to deliver gravel and fill from Cwmynyscoy Quarries, Pontymoile to the construction sites of British Nylon Spinners Pontypool, Uskmouth Power stations and Llanwern Steel Works, working long hours.

Long and Wide Load in Castle Street

Tight squeeze through Castle Street. Looks like someone is going to have a new downpipe! The view of the rear of the large cylinder as it negotiates the Hanbury Inn turn out of Castle Street, heading for the river bridge and Newport Docks.

Looking up Castle Street in the 1920s, a view that is still recognisable today. This is a reproduction of a water colour painting in the style of and attributed to an early 'E.J. Mayberry'.

Castle Street, Caerleon Baptist Church Senior Boys Sunday School Class 1913. Left to right, standing: Jack Williams, Fred James, Percy Ware and Phillip Hills. Seated: Les James, Reg Scannell, Reverend Dewi Bevan Jones (Minister) and Les Hewinson. All the young men served in the 1914-18 War and survived!

Old Time Music Hall with Caerleon Ladies Choir and Albert Harris as *'The Laughing Policeman'*. Left to right ?, ?, Olwen Jones, Rose Hall, Florence Pritchard, Mrs. Perkins and Albert Harris.

A children's participation circus event held in the Town Hall in the 1960s.

Caerleon Scouts and Cub Scouts

Caerleon Cub Scouts marching down Dock Street passing Corn Street Newport after attending the pantomime show *'Puss in Boots'* at the *'Olympia'* Cinema in 1958.

Scout Shield presentation in 1960 at the Scout Hut in Cold Bath Road. Left to right: Jonathan Parker, Nick Niklasson, David Bevan, David Kemp, Johan Voss and Ron Wilson (Scout Leader).

Caerleon and District Fanciers Club

Medals and Commemorative Plates Awards in 1907 and 1928. *'Red Light'* This is to certify that the following positions were taken by M.T. Hewings *'Old Birds'* 8th Ludlow Sweep 51 miles, 1st Chester 107 miles, 4th Shrewsbury 74 miles, 4th Lancaster 166 miles, 15th Rennes Cardiff, SWSRC Open Race 252 miles. Also timed in on third day from *'Marrennes National Race'* 411 miles. President W. Jeremiah Esq., Secretary A.E. Stewart.

Above: the Gold Medals won by G. Edwards, Winner Tynemouth Race in 1928.

Left: *'Red Admiral'* Messrs. Richards Bros. *'Old Birds'* 5th & 7th Ludlow Sweep 53 miles, 6th Shrewsbury 76 miles, 8th Chester 109 miles, 2nd Lancaster 168 miles. President W. Jerimiah Esq., Secretary A.E. Stewart.

Each plate is glazed ceramic and approximately 12 inches in diameter.

Mrs. Betty Vickery's father Graham Edwards in his pigeon loft at the rear of his home at 17 Mill Street circa 1930s.

Albert Harris feeds his feathered friends at his loft at Belmont House where he had a flat.

Home Defence 2nd World War 1939-45

1943 Civil Defence Corp. Caerleon Squad, Decontamination and Heavy Rescue. Back row: Frank Cook, Bert Waters, 'Punch' Marchant, ?, Seth Davies, Arthur Haines, Jack Lewis, Albert Thomas, Arthur Dark, John Mapp, Bert Hill, Jack Harris, Fred Ledger. Front row: Jack Banner, Edwin Batt, Jack Cannon, Squad Leader William Hutchings, Jack Brown, Will Kembrey, Eddie Kembrey. Photograph taken in the grounds of *'Greylands'*, Station Road after a game of bowls. The squad was led by William Hutchings and was based at Cold Bath Road using a former mushroom growing shed as H.Q.. A 3 ton Bedford Lorry (Army) with canopy as a top was provided to carry the heavy lifting and rescue equipment. The driver was Seth Davies, a local farmer who lived and farmed Tan House Farm. Fifteen men manned the hut each night between 2000 hours and 0600 hours. Daytime  cover was given by those hearing the siren, which was installed on top of Cambria House. Those off duty acted as 2nd line group if the first had turned out. During the night hours beds were provided for rest and instant response. Many wooden toys were made during the waking hours using scrap timber. A band saw, carpentry tools etc. were loaned by Bill Hutchings, they even asked for spring steel out of old corsets to make toy tommy guns. All these items were made for sale, monies going towards the *'prisoner of war'* fund. Also made were fun fair rides with dogs, swans, horses etc. on the round-about, which was hand turned from the centre using an Austin 7 differential and mangle wheel and handle.

During the summer evenings those engaged in getting the harvest were allowed to come on duty later. As well as the usual facilities for making tea etc. There was a half-size snooker table, dartboard and card games. Later in the war, moving pictures with sound arrived and were shown in the evening to all members of the public at 6 pence (2½p) one of which was *'Gone with the Wind'* in 8 reels! Also with the fairground was a conventional slide and a *'flying fish'*. which consisted of a long cable raised at one end 3 to 4 metres high and secured at the other end of the ground, down which a seat ride body shaped with wings like a flying fish would carry a child by gravity to be caught at the bottom. No accidents were recorded but it must have been quite a thrill. These fairs later formed the basis of the very popular community *'holidays at home'* weeks.

The ARP also had the use of a four-wheeled GWR platform luggage trolley piled with equipment together with a water bowser hand cart with galvanised buckets for use with stirrup pumps.

BILLETING OFFICER AT CAERLEON

COUNCIL DECISION ON STANDING ORDERS

Caerleon District Council have appointed Mr. H. D. Evans as chief billeting officer.

The Chairman, Mrs. Griffith Jones, J.P., and Councillor W. G. Lovett, Chairman of the A.R.P. Committee, paid a tribute to those who had worked so well and with such unity in connection with billeting and A.R.P work.

Councillor Lovett said they hoped at Caerleon to be 100 per cent. efficient in A.R.P. organisation as soon as possible. Sand bagging, he said, needed speeding up.

He said no one had so far received a penny pay in connection with A.R.P work, and he referred particularly to useful assistance rendered by the Basque boys.

The Council decided, on the motion of Councillor J. Dowden, not to suspend Standing Orders, so that all matters will be dealt with in the usual way by the Council.

Councillor Jacobs suggested that in the event of an emergency meeting, members, where possible, should be notified of the meeting by telephone.

The Chairman said he thought all should have the same opportunity of being informed of any meeting.

Royal British Legion, Caerleon Branch

November 2000, on parade to the Memorial escorted by Air Training Corps Guard of Honour. Left to right: ?, Glyn Evans, Arthur Knorz, Geoffrey McGrath, Edward Cooper, Councillor Jim Kirkwood and Henry West the Poppy Appeal organiser.

They shall not grow old, as we who are left grow old
Age shall not weary them nor the years condemn
At the going down of the sun and in the morning we will
remember them.
When you go home, tell them, for your tomorrows,
we gave our todays.

Massed Legion standards from all over Gwent. David Jones (Caerleon Postmaster) in the centre, in the uniform of an Officer of the Boys Brigade, will carry out the duty of sounding the last post.

Caerleon in Bloom 2000

'Caerleon in Bloom' display of winners' photographs at the August Carnival 2000. Peter Williams reclines and Brian Turner advises and explains.

The 1993-2000 Committee Get Together at the End of Season Lunch at the *'Red Lion'*, Backhall Street in 1999. On the left Norman Stevens, Sue Bennett, Rosemary Butler, Jan Davies, Norma Sturrock and Cliff Suller. On right David Jenkins, Janet Ripley, Bob Roome, Phil Rollings and Margaret Frost. Committee members not present are Peter Williams, Brian Turner, Sue Manship and Councillor Jim Kirkwood.

A Last Look at Caerleon Cricket Club Pavilion and Clubhouse

After more than fifty years the cricket pavilion nears the date for demolition in April 2000. The site is being redeveloped as a Tourist Information Centre with some facilities in its design for cricket club use. On the right the clubhouse of Caerleon Rugby Club. The pavilion was first built in the 1950s and sited near the football club grandstand, it was moved to its final location in 1965 and demolition started in September/October 2000.

CAERLEON CRICKET CLUB

Caerleon Cricket team circa 1960. Seated in the background is Ted Anthony. Back row, left to right: Allan Bamford, Ron Monger, Gordon Murray, John O'Shea, Colin Twine and John Kirk. Seated: Bill Hillier, Roy Langfield, Stuart Watkins, Ivor Davies, (Fly) Harris and Clifford Murray.

Caerleon Cricket Club

Caerleon Cricket team in the 1930s. The college is in the background on the right. Standing is Ernie Jordan. Left to right are C. Evelyn Gough, Bill Lloyd, Bert Waters, George Wall, Fred Bolton, ?. Front row: Henry Pearce, Reg Young, Cliff Sadler and Walter Young.

Caerleon Cricket Club Team in 1949-50. Left to right standing: Ray Greenway, Tom Davies, Glyn Nolmes, Arthur Webber, Don Lewis, Alan Jones and John Stewart. Seated: Bert Waters, Jack Powell, Don Stewart, Stan Vickery, Bill Hillier and Dick Stewart.

Opening the new season in 1974 with the Mayor of Newport bowling the jack to start the first game. Councillor John Marsh with Mayoress Mrs. Marion Marsh in the centre foreground Councillor Rosemary Butler C.U.D.C., and Max Morrish the Town Clerk.

Formed in 1964 the Ladies Section of Caerleon Bowling Club in 1985. Left to right: Gwen Lamb, Mrs. Francis, Ada Milliner, Mrs. Kathleen Warren the Mayoress of Newport, Florence Asquith, Martha (Jane) Knorz and Mayor of Newport, Councillor Trevor Warren.

Caerleon A.F.C. Circa 1950

Caerleon Second Team. Back row, left to right: ?, Arthur Knorz, Ken (Ikey) Miles, Reg Johnson, Herbert Davies, Ray Greenaway, Ron Parry, ? and B. Treharne. Front row: Royston Hill, John Waggett, Harold Phillips, ? and Allan Jones.

Caerleon Football Team and Committee in 1951. Standing, left to right: Peter Ledger, Les Hubbard, Ken (Ikey) Miles, Ken Anstee, John Kembrey, Les Nash, Jack Fletcher, Jimmy Dixon, Alan Jones, Dennis White, Grenville Anstee and Tommy Davies. Seated: Cecil Watts, Eddie Nash, President George Mill, Lou Lewis and Don Stewart the Honorary Secretary.

Caerleon Rugby Club

A presentation in 1980 to Andrew Rice the *'Most Promising Player'* by Councillor Rosemary Butler.

The picture below shows how he confirmed his promising start by being selected for the first team.

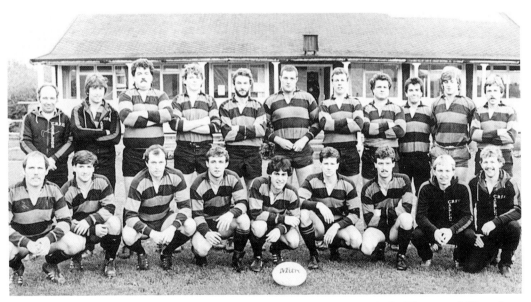

Caerleon RFC 1984-85. Back row, left to right: R. Rice (Trainer), D. Thomas, J. Vizard, T. Derrett, R. O'Donnell, A. Jones, M. Lewis, J. Jones, P. Thomas, M. Davies and R. Derrett. Front row: P. Macey, S. Roberts, G. McCarthy, A. Rice, D. Powell, G. Gwynne, M. Sutton, S. Dominy and A. Wood.

'Ashwell Villa'

The original *'Ash Well Villa'* built in the 1800s as a farm house and named after the ash tree and well nearby. It was demolished in around 1935. The house came to the edge of the roadway, this area is now front gardens.

Built in the rear garden of the original house in the late 1930s are two pairs of semi detached houses. The builder used a great deal of the dressed stone from the demolition to construct them. The ground floor walls are of extraordinary thickness, some of the remainder of the dressed stone was used to border the front garden paths. Digging in the garden over the years has turned up relics of past occupation such as pieces of decorated Victorian floor tile, a three-inch-high doll figure of a Welsh Lady wearing an apron and holding a leek, made in white Parian ware. A child's teapot with lid, and a one and half inch high Parian ware pig, playing a violin. A clay pipe bowl with Erin Harp motif and three-leaf clover design embossed presumed not lost by a little girl!

Mary Broomfield's birthday party at *'The Grange'*, Isca Road in 1923. Pictured are Mrs. Langsmaid and son, Mrs. Lewis and Neville, Mrs. Broomfield and Mary, David Buck and Mrs. Buck, Beryl Arnold, Peter Buck, Graham Jones, Miss Young, Billie Meyrick-Williams, Molly Phillips, Gabrielle ? and Mr. Buck seated in the car.

Front garden of the new Ashwell Villa in 1952. Pictured are Christine Lavender, Michael Holder, Ted Lavender, Diane Jenkins, Brenda Lavender, Jeremy Holder and Caroline Lavender. A springtime afternoon that was spent gathering bluebells at Wentwood.

Ultra Pontem and Ashwell Carnival in 1952

Society Lady, Mother's Ruin and a Tropical Island Maiden. Left to right are John Porter, Ted Lavender and Tom Holder.

Ultra Pontem and Ashwell Carnival in August 1952. 'Ashwell' for many years held a separate carnival in the field behind No.3 Ashfield Villas owned by the Lavender family. All children had a memento as a gift and pensioners were entertained with a meal in the marquee. Everyone except the pensioners dressed up. Pictured are Christine Lavender (The Nun), Caroline Lavender (Queen of Hearts), Brenda Lavender (Wee Willy Winkie), Ted Lavender (Old Mother Riley), Tom Holder (South Sea Maiden) and John Porter. Monies to fund the carnival were raised by the community collecting scrap iron which was stored in front gardens until it was taken to a yard in Pontypool. A total of £30 was raised.

Coronation of Queen Elizabeth II in 1953

All the family dining chairs have been commandeered. A very festive occasion with bunting and trees in full bloom contributed to a memorable day. Each child received a commemorative silver plated mug with a medallion of the queen's head embossed on it in gold as their souvenir.

A bright sunny June afternoon to celebrate the Coronation with a street party at 'Ashwell'. Left to right Christine Lavender, Caroline Lavender and local children.

An Aspect of the Sporting Life of Ultra Pontem

The 'Badger Club' of Ultra Pontem taken at Wentwood Forest in 1938. As seen in the picture on the left there was plenty of cider in stone jars and a case of bottled beer. The club disbanded in 1939 with the outbreak of war and was not re-formed. Meetings were held at the Bell Inn. Back row, left to right 'Buster' Williams, Bob Hoskins, Stan Vickery, Jim Cook, ?, Cyril Phillips and Alan Jenkins. Front row: Arthur Vickery, Jim Tooze, David Cook, Ebenezer Cook and Bert Pattemore.

Springtime, rear of the 'Great House', Isca Road, circa 1930.

Valley of the 'Usk River' in April 1998. Looking from St. Julian's pub Ashwell and Ultra Pontem to the right with the Ship Inn and Malthouse Hotel to the centre and Hanbury Arms Inn left of the bridge. A superb scenic photograph by the late E.G. (Eddie) Moss of Newport.

Green Remembered Hills by Dennis W. Heslop

Caerleon Town close to Newport, a most attractive sight, long and narrow green it has, pubs to the left and right. 'Genteel' now the pubs we knew, all modernised and 'flash'. No more spit 'n' sawdust or having to go outside for a ....!

Great Roman legions marched there once, many traces still to see, also temple, theatre and many sites of great antiquity.

Take the road leads down to Usk, towards old 'Twin Oaks' mill, passing through look up to your right, St. Albans on the hill. Both have gone now sad to say, the mill a new estate, St. Albans House turned into a drinking den burned down one dark night, late!

Those lovely hills though still can you see clothed as ever in greening tree, fast River Usk remains on course winding wild and free through its daisied meadows in wide and lush valley.

Port of Newport on southern side spreading tentacles ever wide, once had old buildings fine galore, most alas sadly destroyed now to delight no more! All the same there still remains some old sights to see. Castle, market, transporter bridge (can one still ride it free).

Sad day though in '74 when Monmouth Shire was no more, romantic notions now seem spent since those narrow minded renamed it Gwent.

– – – – – – – –

Dennis Wade Heslop, brother of Elsie Gibbens (Twin Oaks Sawmills), called up by the Royal Navy and served from 1944 to 1948. He trained as an officers' steward at HMS Royal Arthur, on completion served at sea aboard the destroyer HMS Zest aged 19 years.

A prolific writer he had three poems published and he was invited to the USA to the *'International Society of Poets'* in Washington D.C. in June 1947. He developed a great love of the Caerleon area and worked as an accountant to the General Medical Council in London. He was born in 1926 and died in 1997.

Acknowledgements

For photographs, time, advice, information, useful assistance and constructive criticism! I readily give my sincere thanks, without you nothing could be achieved.

John Abraham (Newport City Library), Mrs. Lily Avery, Gino Alonzi, South Wales Argus, Bob Atkins (Newport RFC), Mike Buckingham (S.W. Argus), Val Burnell-Jones, Doug and Beryl Burnell-Higgs, Rosemary Butler (AM Assembly of Wales), Jane Bray (P.I.F.A. Monmouth Archaeology), John and Joan Bevan, Rose Bowen, Marjorie Bennett, Linda Bisby, Butterley Engineering (Ripley Derby), Jeff Bishop, Julie Baxter, Edward Besly (National Museum of Wales), Nigel Blackmore M.A., (Roman Legion Museum), Dr. Wynford Bellin (Colinston, Cowbridge), David Bevan, Joe Beddow, Matthew Brookner, S. Coombes B.Ed. (Lodge Hill Infants School), Stephen Clarke, M.B.E., F.S.A., M.I.F.A. (Monmouth Archaeology), Wallace Cochran (Ponthir), Bryn Collier (Ponthir), Roger Cooksey (Keeper of Fine Art, Newport City Museum), Edna Carter, Charles and Margery Cryans, Rosalie Davies, Paul Dixon (Caerleon College), John Derret, Seth (Cecil) Davies, Tommy Davis, Molly Davies, Don and Irene Dodd (Croesyceiliog), Douglas Davies, Allan Dowling (Caldicot), Peta Davies (nee Coopey), David Eagles, Kirston Elliot (Western Mail & Echo), Will Evans (Newport), Darren Evans (S.W. Argus), Donna Evans (nee Pugh), Reverend Canon Arthur Edwards, B.A., M.Phil., Phill George (Station Officer S.W. Fire Service), Elsie Gibbens, Royce Gardener (retired Sheriff of Caerleon), Enrique Garay, Edward Gibbens, Ken Graham, Allan Grant, Mrs. V. Gough, David Gregort (Ashwell), Reverend Claire Griffiths, Margaret Harper, Jamie Harper, Dr. and Mrs. E.E. Hewinson M.B., C.H.B. (Ponthir), Ronald Hewinson (Newport), Doreen Harris (Ponthir), Audrey Hemmings, Catherine Hawke, Frank Harding B.A., B.ed. (retired Head Teacher Lodge Hill Junior School), Dawn Hoar (Pavis), Denise Jones (Bassaleg), David and Carole Jones (Caerleon Post Office), Emlyn Jones (Legion Museum), Jean James (Caerleon Library), Richard Jones (Pontypool), Margaret Jones, Allan Jones (Newport), James Kirkwood, F.R.S.A. (Councillor Newport City), Arthur Knorz (Cwmbran), Cliff V. Knight (Newport), Pam Kilvington, Edith Lewis (Usk), Neil Leyland (S.W. Fire Service), Brenda Lavender, Elizabeth Luck, Eric Ledger, Mark Lewis B.Sc., M.Sc. (Legion Museum), Kathleen Morgan, Gwyneth Miles, Jen and John Moore (Pontypool), Edney Moss (Photographer Newport), Mike McLeur (Newport), Anne Maloney, Lynette Morris, Raymond Marasco (Newport), Monmouthshire Railway Society, Nigel Miggens, Gordon Murray Assistant Curate, Reverend Clare Mitchell B.A., Dpt., Newport City Reference Library Staff, Eddie Niklasson, Pauline O'Sullivan, the late Ron Pearce, Ralph Peacock (Grimsby), Christopher Perks (Bristol), George and Pat Pincher, Jim and Pamela Phelps (Bishops Stortford), John Pritchard B.Sc. (Hons.) (Newport City Council), Sylvia Parsons (Caerleon Library), Howard Pell (Cwmbran), Sonia Phillips (Langstone), Jim and Jackie Povall, Victor Romero (Spain - Caerleon College), Mrs. R.A. Richards, Lyn Richards, Ken Rees, Phil Rollings, Dr. Russell Rees, M.D., Gillian Rees, William Roberts, David and Kath Rushton, Stephanie Rollings, Keith and Caroline Richards (Cwmbran), David Reynolds B.A. (Lodge Junior School), Ray and Brenda Raines, Pendre Sims (S.W. Argus), Fred Salmon (Newport), Gerald Strongman (Henllys), Miguel Santiago (Priory Hotel), Phil Stobart (Western Mail & Echo), Edna May Strong, the late Don Stewart, Carole Stevens, Steve Strong, Josephine Savery (nee Alvarez - Risca), Sidney Shaw, Anne Sterry, Glyn Teague, Bob Trett (Caerleon History Tours), Felicity Taylor (Monmouth Archaeology), Doreen Trickey (Llanhenock), R. Jeremy Taylor (Barnt Green, W. Midlands), Brian and Sue Underwood, Tracy Tanner (nee Pugh), Doreen Vickery, Marilyn Woolley, Wilfred Wilson (Artist), Lyndon and June Watts (Stafford), Patrick White (Newport), www.caerleon.net, Henry West, Jim and Queenie Waggett, Steve Wilmott (Usk), Derek Williams, Tom Whiteley (S.W. Argus), Roger Williams (Pen-y-Wain Farm), William Wookey, W. Howard Wookey, Anthony Wood, Paul and Stephanie Winterfeld, Megan Williams, Nigel Young, David Zeinkowitz (Legion Museum).

To Dr. Russell Rees for his kindness in providing the foreword, my thanks also to Malcolm Thomas and all the staff at Old Bakehouse Publications for their friendly helpful advice and encouragement. To the Caerleon residents, your interest in the project is overwhelming my grateful thanks and so to the next one!

Books, Newspapers, Magazines consulted
Bibliography

Guide to Caerleon-on-Usk - W.A. Morris. Lt. Col. RAMC retired. Pub. 1931.

Newport Directories - R.H. Johns 1899, 1908.

Great Western Railway, Ticket Examiners, Current (1928) Fares Book

Caerleon Heritage Trail - Pamphlet published by Caerleon Civic Society, Caerleon Local History Society and Gwent County Council

'Historic Caerleon' A Walk Around - Pamphlet published by Caerleon Civic Society, research by P. Hockey

'Caerleon - Isca' - Roman Legionary Museum Booklet, Pub. 1987, National Museum of Wales

'A Popular Guide to Caerleon' - by ISCA and Atwood Thorne M.B. (Lond.). Pub. 1928. Western Mail Ltd.

South Wales Argus - Various Dates

Souvenir Programme Sat 13th June, 1987 to celebrate the opening of the Roman Legionary Museum

'Hanbury Ale House' - Information Pamphlet 1996.

'Historic Caerleon' - Official Guide of the Urban District Council 1955.

Monmouthshire County Guide 1954 - Pub. Mon. C.C. by the Home Publishing Co., Croydon

The Story of Brynglas House - by D.L. Anne Hobbs, Research by Tony Friend. Pub. by Brynglas Community Educational Centre 1989.

'Steam in South Wales Volume 4' - Monmouthshire by Michael Hale, Pub. Oxford Pub. Co.

History of the Red Cross in Monmouthshire 1920-1918 - by Robin Jones R.G.N., A.I.C.D. Pub. 1988

The Roman Past of Heidenheim and its Twin Towns - by Helmut Weimert. Pub. Heidenheim City Archives 1991

'Newport Transport' 80 Years of Service - E.A. Thomas.

Caerleon Past and Present - Primrose Hockey M.B.E.

Caerleon Endowed Schools 1724-1983 - T.M. Morgan. Pub. Starling Press 1983.

Caerleon Endowed Schools 'The First 270 Years' - T.M. Morgan. Pub. Williams Schools Caerleon

'On The Track of the Caerleon Tramroad - by Kirsten Elliot and Andrew Swift. *'Archive'* Magazine No.32. Published by *'Archive'*, 47-49 High Street, Lydney, Gloucestershire GL15 5DD

'Caerleon Roman Amphitheatre' - by Sir Mortimer Wheeler and Dr. V.E. Nash Williams F.S.A. Pub. by Welsh Office Official Handbook 1970.

'Roman Trail Guide' - by Howard Pell.

'Portraits of the Past' - by Chris Barber and Michael Blackmore. Pub. Blorenge Books.